With love and the mem<del>ory of a reading</del> in the <del>back</del>
room at Prairie Lights on Sept. 20, 1991

— DJ

# What I Think I Know

*Other Books by Robert Dana*

POETRY

*Starting Out for the Difficult World*, 1987
*In a Fugitive Season*, 1980
*The Power of the Visible*, 1971
*Some Versions of Silence*, 1967

PROSE

*Against the Grain: Interviews with Maverick
　　　　American Publishers*, 1986

LIMITED EDITIONS

*Blood Harvest*, 1986
*What the Stones Know*, 1982
*In a Fugitive Season*, 1979
*Journeys from the Skin*, 1966 (pamphlet)
*The Dark Flags of Waking*, 1964
*My Glass Brother and Other Poems*, 1957 (pamphlet)

# What I Think I Know

*Robert Dana*

New &
Selected Poems

Robert Dana

*another chicago press*
*another chicago press*
*another chicago press*
*another chicago press*
*another chicago press*
*another chicago press*
*another chicago press*
*another chicago press*
*another chicago press*
*another chicago press*
*another chicago press*
*another chicago press*
*another chicago press*

Copyright © 1991 Robert Dana

All Rights Reserved

Published in the United States by Another
Chicago Press, Box 11223, Chicago, IL 60611

Cover painting "August in Detroit" © 1991 by
Edward Levine

Poems from the following previously published
books are included in this volume of New &
Selected Poems:

*My Glass Brother and Other Poems,* copyright
©1957 by Robert Dana; originally published by
The Constance Press, later The Stone Wall Press.

*Some Versions of Silence,* copyright ©1967 by
W. W. Norton; 1986 by Robert Dana.

*The Power of the Visible,* copyright ©1971 by
Robert Dana.

*In a Fugitive Season,* copyright ©1979, 1980 by
Robert Dana; published in limited edition by
The Windhover Press of The University of Iowa,
and in trade edition by The Swallow Press of
The University of Ohio (Athens).

*Starting Out for the Difficult World,* copyright
©1987 by Robert Dana. Parts of this book were
published in limited editions under the titles
*Blood Harvest* and *What the Stones Know* by
The Windhover Press of The University of Iowa
and by The Seamark Press; the trade edition was
published by Harper & Row.

This project is funded in part by generous grants
from the Illinois Arts Council and the National
Endowment for the Arts.

Library of Congress
Catalog Card Number: 90-85016

ISBN: 0-929968-18-2

Distributed exclusively by
Independent Literary Publishers
Association, PO box 816,
Oak Park, IL 60303

*for those whose voices have not been heard*

# CONTENTS

*. . . poetry is the orphan of silence.*

Charles Simic

*We tell ourselves stories in order to live.*

Joan Didion

# Words for My Wife

When, at the last, my sun
Blunders down
To darkness, the bright shout
Of air will freeze to silence on the bone;
The blood's strict latitudes will be undone;
And I'll wash out
Through the easy music of my skin,
As I once came in.

Of what remains, take care.
It's what I had,
A loveliness of nerves.
It whispered me into shapes of the blue world,
And I found myself. There is no everywhere.
Each small life curves
To its own shimmer, clothing the known
Like a bird or stone.

Water was my element;
My law, motion.
When tides plucked at me,
I sailed. There are no maps of that lost region
Behind the eye. The moon, where my wake bent,
Printed the sea
With fire, and the beat of dark loam
Guided me home.

Remember, then, when all
My fury lies

*In a heap of scars, how*
*I lived. Keep me from the shattering kiss*
*Of fire and the immemorial worm's soft call.*
*Sweet wife, speak low,*
*And commend my body to the deep,*
*That I may sleep.*

# My Glass Brother And Other Poems
## (1957)

# Pop: at Checkers

I see you, boy, crouched behind your eyes,
Biting your bitter Irish mouth. You lean
Above the board where my one red king flies
Before your black, half stranger to me still.
I hear the armored june-bugs beat the screen;
      Hot cars grind up the hill;
"Your move," you say again. My mind adrift,
I watch the lines of checkers break and shift.

Four years back you came to live with me,
Your body hollowed to the bone with hate,
Sick of the cold clothes of charity.
You seldom spoke. You kept to your attic room,
With blazing knucklebreakers, a stolen skate,
      And a Fokker red as doom.
And all that spring, pajamas wet to the seams,
Fighting my arms, you woke from savage dreams.

What could I say? When your mother died,
Your dapper salesman father hit the road.
Who could blame you for your crooked pride?
But here, boy, all that is is gut-wrung, had
By body-breaking labor. We know the load
      We bear. The lights of sad
Farms and failing mills burn late. Each gear
And valve whistles back the cramp of fear.

Night is deepening, and the moon has set.
Double-jumping, you take my pawn and king

And smile. Beyond our game, beyond the fret
Of weary bookkeepers, dark countries sleep,
And guttural, heavy bombers are readying
          Tomorrow. Love won't keep.
Boy, across this checkered no-man's land,
Speak my name, reach out and touch my hand.

# A Winter's Tale

It is a winter night. Fever and chill
Rummage the blind cars on Lover's Hill,
And rabbits shiver in the frozen grass.
Along the river, ice, like broken glass,
Clicks and flickers. For an hour we walk
The bank, and I half listen to your talk
Of kids and marriage. Here, piles of junk
Blaze with frost, and summer's juice is sunk
To the hidden root. But even as a bloom
Of ice melts in my hand, I think of a room
Warmed by summer moonlight. You are beside
Me on the bed. I turn. Your eyes grow wide
And darken as we kiss. Wild and sweet,
Your body whispers against me on the sheet.
But this is dream; for I have heard the west
Wind sigh down the dozing Berkshires, its past
Naming our future, the tide of its restlessness
Heaving through raw towns. It is not less
Than itself, this image. It summons me
Where breakneck houses spill toward a fresh sea.
And you, you are your father's child; your face
Tells me you will never leave this place,
His dead mills, the hope that they'll come back
To life. Downstream, they loom, crusted wrack
jamming their floodgates, their bobbins wound
With the dust of years. Watchman and hound
Prowl the yards. But what is there to watch?
Tonight, your father warms his hopes with Scotch,
And pacing before the fireplace, stops, and turns

To stare at *The Wall Street Journal* as it burns.
Now, the town clock bells you home. But I
Draw you close. You smile a little and cry
Against my shoulder. We stand in this heavy air,
And stand, knowing all we'll ever share
Is this embrace. The sky above us palls,
And the blue snow melts about us as it falls.

# My Glass Brother

When I was five and distant from immense
Black Africas of thought, you held your peace.
My Eden world behind the picket fence
Stood wished and real; the wind of its increase
Fed gently at the tree of innocence.
Our mother's death revoked my stubborn lease.
And you, your exile broken, cast the dies,
Twin continents dimensioned in your eyes.

At twelve, the mongrel age, when confidence
Is cock and bull, I sulked unsatisfied.
Across that vast inch of adolescence,
Their bodies tight with mystery and pride,
The girls whose silent promise raids your presence
passed with ruthless, unrelenting stride.
I cursed them for a pack of bitches, yet,
A subtle fever nagged my palms with sweat.

It was my eighteenth year: I was the rage
Of Guam, the slickest bull-shit artist in the fleet,
And sick for home. I made my pilgrimage
To Apra's Seven Sisters. On the drunken street,
The Shore Patrol, and in the swinging cage
The parrot chants a litany: dead-beat,
Dead-beat, the great Pacific fleet is sunk—
That night they found me screaming in my bunk.

Now, the nurses glide along the hall;
The ward is quiet. You and I, old pros,

Need no game of hearts or stud to stall
The coming of the night. Winter sows
Its seed upon the garden and the softball
Field behind your face. It drifts and blows
Around the vision that my years have earned:
Two trees, black—and a love-seat overturned.

# For Sister Mary Apolline

*"'How good,' he thinks, 'that she breathes in*
*oblivion with every breath she draws! That in*
*childhood each night is a deep gulf between one*
*day and the next.'"*
*Thomas Mann, "Disorder and Early Sorrow"*

## I

Now, wrangling bells discipline the day
And the doves, in frenetic scramble, flee
Their steeples. I watch them blown like debris
Over the wind-tormented roofs of town.
On the schoolgrounds, amid children hot for play,
Sisters stroll. You, my sister, hands
A-clapping, scold a wild disorder down.
One small boy meets your challenge eye
To eye. Who knows from that tall glance
what bells may ring, and what doves fly?

## II

When I called "Sister" half the convent turned
And smiled; children touched my blues,
Awed by the bells that swung above my shoes.
I paused, a stranger, in the scuffled dust.
This is a child's world. Here, where love is learned,
You turn to gamy ends these endless days;

Meg jumps rope and only Bob who's lost
His ball knows the size and shape of grief
You fall to me and we embraced. In your gaze
I saw the season, blossom, blade, and leaf.

### III

Sister, we share no common heritage.
A son who does not wear his father's name,
My birth engendered all; the public shame
That rattled mother screwloose in her bed;
Your father, shattering in his rage
The sideboard glass, the radio, and the clock;
Your trembling prayers, and your bowed head.
Above my crib dry birds of paper twirled,
And I, startled by the sounds, the shock,
Woke weeping in the dark and adult world.

### IV

When, at seventeen, you took the veil,
I walked and whistled in a Berkshire wood;
As small boys sometimes can, I understood.
Where Christ, half frozen, legs like sticks,
Hangs in some convent shrine by a rusty nail,
You pray our sins away and ask for grace
And bruise your knees upon the winter bricks.
I am the State's child, now. Being alone
Is something I know better than my face.
The path I walk leads everywhere but home.

### V

In those islands of the wise, the Solomons,
The sea salutes the exile. It's Christmas eve;

Drunk as lords, the port side dreams of leave
Tonight, and we, our tin cups full of Scotch,
Drink the bloody health of all men's sons.
We carol out of time and out of tune.
Forward, the bos'n bells the starboard watch,
And half the night we watch gulls wheel and flee
Our threatening shape across the moon,
Down the never and forever changing sea.

## VI

Now, day's last light dies in the pebbled yard,
And the manic winds of March betray the season.
We stop and listen. The bells, sound without reason,
Summon the sailor seaward, the nun to prayer.
Where there is time, time is its own reward.
We say goodbye. I turn and go, but stay
Fixed forever in your parting stare.
Eastward, the darkness that the doves are bringing;
But in the street, a boy prolongs his play,
Now murmuring to himself, now softly singing.

Some Versions of Silence
(1967)

# Late Fall Zinnias

*for my son*

Early evening. No
Wind. A frost snapping
In the late blue light.
The last leaves fallen,
Burning, make the tent
Of fire we camp by.

Some things we live by.
This garden where no
Vine bears now, intent
On winter: snapping
Pods: seeds fallen
Toward another light.

On my lap you're light,
A ripe burr of boy
Stuck, where you've fallen,
With mud. What you know:
Delight in snapping
Coals, a bright content.

You sense the extent
Of darkness, and light
Only draws you. By
It, colors snapping,

Zinnias say "no"
To the frost fallen.

Praise these unfallen
Then, tough-stemmed, intent.
Pick, and hold them. No
Emblem is slight.
Roots are to hold by
When all is snapping.

Wind rises, snapping.
You sit there, fallen
Asleep, flowers by.
I pick you up; tend
The fire into light,
Doing what I know

How to. On distant
Yards, our sparks light:
Firebirds on black snow.

# Waiting

He sits there.

      A window fills with
the stillness of birds.

He's waiting

      for something. Something
to happen. Some one.

For some word

      from someone. But his
door is a wall. His

lights are out.

      No one can reach him.
No word possibly

can reach him.

      Perhaps the waiting
itself brings him what

he waits for.

      Perhaps his waiting
is all that happens.

Or perhaps

      the black lightning of
      branches, the green sky

are the words.

# A Note from Nowhere

I have thought
much of you,

my brother,
my sister.

I write now
only to

say
          spiders
drown in milk.

Each day its
own season,

so storms of
flowers move.

Jays at my
feeder claim

no more than
their own shapes.

Over and
over.
          And

between us
silence has

a sound we
never gave

it.
        Nothing
is. Is real.

## Lost/Found

First,
he looked
for himself
in documents,
in fouled
certificates
he knew
to be his,
on which
his name
never appeared.

Then,
in books,
where he found
only what
he might
become,
always under
another name.

Then,
amid weather,
animals;
and once
in the body
of a dead
honeybee
perfect

on the sub-zero
snow.

    And
finally
in the faces
of others,
in their eyes,
which he found
empty
as they
beheld him.

# A Letter from Divizio, Patient, Pilgrim State Hospital

"Dear Friends,"
You begin.

But we don't know
You, Joseph Divizio.

Unless you're
The man we glimpsed
Once, from our stalled
Commuter, the one
Homburged and gloved
In authority,
Hailing a cab
For Madison Ave.,
58th, or Wall.

Now, you tell
Us you're a graduate
Of NYU,
A civil servant,
A member of Life
Study Fellowship,
American, white,
And not sick;
That you were abducted
By conspirators,
You, Divizio.

You say we must
Fire those who aided,
Abetted your abduction;
We must restore
Your liberty,
Your money; restore
You, Divizio,
To your wife, Betty,
Née Del Bello;
We must bring legal
And other aid.

Years ago,
Was it you we heard
At the back of the tour,
When an old wino,
Hawking his undershirt
Like pity, touched
The disgust of our sleeves,
And a woman snickered.
Was it your voice,
Said audibly, "Shit"?

We don't know
You, Joseph Divizio,
Nor the fellow
"Prisoners" you name,
The "undesireables":
Not Maddi, Tirrado,
Tolman White
(Negro); not
Shick Hernandez,
Nor Medina, nor Imperial.

Though you know our town,
Our street, our number.

Though you sign yourself
"Yours, Joseph
Divizio, Joseph
Lawrence Divizio."

# The Power of the Visible
## (1971)

# The Unbroken Code

Agent of obscure
powers, countries whose names, whose
locations even, he

cannot now recall.
As he cannot distinguish,
some days, his real

from his coded name.
Or say why he carries that
map of broken veins

inside his ankle.
Who no longer knows he cares,
or cares if he knows

where its roads may lead.
His contact missed, dead perhaps,
he waits for someone

to speak the word he
will remember the ring of,
key to his reason

for being there on
the cheap brass bed by the phone,
in the soaking dark

of *Playa del Sol.*

# Fever

Heat licks the lips
Their bones are fuses
of dry sparks

There is no name
they must guard
their mouths against

Their eyelids close
upon soreness
Sleep deafens them

They do not see
moonlight slide
across cold metal

They see nothing
Nights dissolve
into glasses of water

Days flicker
into the backs
of drawn shades

This is their kingdom
They are its black priests
and sick of it

## Merlin, at the End

He'd spoken the words once.
He still remembered them,
harsh and clear as acid,
how the first word wakened
the air to a fine edge:
pain in a brilliant mirror.

And he thought he saw again
the queen's love darken
into habit for her friend,
and beside the lake, crushed
under the bloody iron,
the king dazzling toward death.

The second word opened
into a silence like sound:
the voice of Vivian, dressed
in green, beside the fountain,
holding in her arms
all there was of darkness.

She turned away singing,
the motion of her hands
set to the world's turning.
Then, there remained only
blackbirds, flowers, the hushed
dome of water falling.

The last word struck

daylight from a white country
he'd never before imagined,
where his skin clung to him
like a jacket and gloves of ice.
And he saw that he was old.

To speak again there, to shake
from the air foreknowledge of acts
neither desired nor understood
lay still within his power,
he knew. And overhead
the sky pointed nowhere.

# A Page of *Changes*

Shutting a door
is called "earth."

Opening a door
is called "heaven."

One door closing
after one opening

after one closing
is called "change."

Some doors are walls.
And some windows.

This is called
"The way it is."

# Picking It Up

## 1

His center lost
for the moment,
he drowns beside
the swimming pool,

reads red letters
and white reversed
on blue:
        *Warning—*
*No Lifeguard On*

*Duty.*
      As he
sinks again in
the plunging sun,
he thinks,

         "What would
you take from me
that, willingly,
I would not give?"

## 2

This other, this
opposite coast?
Belled and gulled,

too.
like the other?

Near, far bells, and
gull's cries among
boats.
                The houses,
the white houses

stacked in tumbles
of streets to the
bay.
        Leafed out like
unbundled knives.

3

This one's silence,
love? That one's, hate?

That one, his days
of poisons spread
in cool hallways,

stillnesses quick
with trip-wires, mines
of his passions.

Or this one, by
a window hurt
with stars, still as

her reasons are
behind her eyes.

4

For this,
       for these,
he lifts the skin
from words his mind
would be made of.

Comes back to sun
making itself
a ring of shade
for three children.

It is not for
luck,
      for nothing,
he touches stone.

# The Stone Garden

At last, he had to
make it with his hands: of earth,
stone, wood trusted to.

Not so different
from things he'd already done.
Another matter.

So he cleared the ground.
Skeletal brown barberry,
limp spirea, weeds

close to the house, he
cut away and later burned.
Rugs of sod he rolled

up to be laid down
elsewhere, not to be wasted.
He worked in the heat

each day, leveling
the earth as his neighbors watched.
Sometimes, resting on

the shaded front steps,
he closed his eyes to enjoy
the wind's Westminster

in the small brass chimes,

or played with his cat, or licked
his own fantastic

salt from his tired arms.
But already he could see
by the corner pine

the low, curving wall
he'd crack a ton of limestone
into, junipers

spraying over it
green, greener than seawater.
And he'd start again.

He laid wall and built
redwood frames to cut the ground
to three even squares,

six odd rectangles.
Spaces to be filled, some with
a blue-grey roadstone

or red bark, and one
with white crushed marble. And one,
by moonlight, he filled

with smooth Japanese
shadows. There, in the night wind,
dried in his own sweat,

he saw clearly how
pale flagstones floated on sand
pieced out a puzzle

the instant before
the pattern falls together,
how they held it there.

By morning, it seemed
still another thing: hard, small
flowers in the sun.

He was hungry then
and went in: to breakfast, to
deaths in the papers.

# The Lie

Early morning light like wine
A high thin clear bouquet
And two small birds
whose cries he could remember
which she'd never heard before so far from water
which sharpened it
And beyond the runway evergreens

In his arms she smelled sweet as promise
They said nothing
admitting they'd lied to themselves for years

Then her plane lifted her away
shearing off south
over its own little-bird shadow
the sun
hanging its warmth in her left ear

He thinks of the drive eastward
he must make without her
of the rivers
the little bells and funeral parlors of small towns
spring gasping warmly in the willows

By evening in that city
he's the complete stranger standing by his motel
Sweet veils of rain
pass in succession up the highway

There's a word for the darkness he feels shining up
But neither of them believes it

# The Way We Live Now

The windows
look back into themselves
through the grey rain

And the bells of the university
sound only a tune

You could say
this house is the ghost of one
you used to live in

where you still put on the future every morning
as shaven jaws

At breakfast
the woman you married
beats like a black hole

the edge of the edge

her flowered blouse
emptying into space like a form of algebra

and suicide is a bright bird
perching on your finger

You whistle to it
and it whistles back

a canary

singing its throat out like a brook
The trickle of blood in a vein

You could say
you're a liar a thief and a compulsive seducer

That this is the way
we live now

# Passage

*for K. K.*

Pigs blister the hillside
And it is doubtless in the sky's color
to burn incredibly.

Morning may strike us anywhere.

So that passing these woods,
seeing orders nailed to fenceposts,
to ruined trees,
we may feel ourselves made strangers,
willing to stop.

We may find ourselves
in suit, dress shoes, and hat
getting out of the car,
taking a walk
where we have no business at all.

We may even recall passing earlier
a farm-wife in slacks and a dead sweater
dragging behind her
the body of her dog.

Or the two roans and a grey
grazing an open slough.

Overhead an unseen bomber
unzips the blue bag of the sky.
In offices,
in the kitchens of farmhouses,
the torn edge of the day curls.

And only the scattered remains of calendars
will be believed.

In a Fugitive Season
(1979)

# In a Fugitive Season

What we know, we discover.
The breath freezes. Leaves fall up.
The sheriff's ducks are on the river.

Winter is never over,
whether I love you or not.
Such thoughts are only the mind's waver,

its senseless bright endeavor
to bring the world to a stop.
But the sheriff's ducks are on the river.

And licks of the sun's fever.
Butter melting in a cup.
Whatever we know, we discover.

From the bridge, we lean over,
letting the stale bread-scraps drop.
Logic is only the mind's waver.

Only the chilled mind's waver.
What we know, we discover:
our faces aswim in the swift clip.
The sheriff's ducks are on the river.

# Summer in a Very Small Town

The small towns of the strange middle of our lives
remain small

Streets wintry
even in summer

Here the old forget themselves in their own stories
the moon rises
a tall tower lifts its silver planet of water into the sky

and the children believe in God
and the cold gardens of his weather

What makes of such poor wisdom
the knife of the will
of such poverty the flower without memory

we do not know

Tonight men wire their bodies to grenades
jets sizzle blind from the deck of carriers
In the streets something dies

If our heads flamed here once
If together we rolled
and the sun rolled
like a pride of lions through the summer grass
and our teeth clicked with a fever
it was another world

where the day was called by your name and mine
and love was another name for sight

Now the cat stirs beside me
in the deep hair of its sleep
and my envy stirs
that last of my rights
even that frail mania

Too far arrived to go back
I see that I am what I always was

that ordinary man on his front steps
bewildered under the bright mess of the heavens
by the fierce indecipherable language of its stars

# The Woman on the Mall

That morning
is only as you remember it
imperfectly

And a woman
walks the green mall lightly
in her light summer dress

She is neither the woman
who started toward you
nor she who will finally arrive

At your window
the first white insects of winter
sting the glass

# The Winter and the Snow

Nothing sharpened his days
The winter and the snow
the snow in successive ripples successive waves
cresting into scarps by the roadside wire
The winter and the snow
The sun on the snow in the broken encampments of
                    stalks
His fields burning like white phosphorous

Nothing sharpened his days
He was nothing he'd imagined
nights the fire kneeled into itself in the darkened room
It surprised him in the act of completeness
that the body is god's fool the fool his library
The winter and the snow

Nothing
A season of minimums
Beyond the end-table
where her nameless houseplant flourished in a clay vase
they cling even to spring in patches scattered like forty
                    years
the winter and the snow

# Moving

Sunlight off the snow

snow frozen and thawed and frozen again
to this silver mesh

The road is like iron meal
where his boots feed

He's walking out on his ambitions
danger in his pockets and the wind close

following the tangled winter edge
of some nerve in his head

under the high pines
past the lake
its still open water shining and black as a collapsed star
into the distance where the crow barks its warning

Where whatever is true
everything falls that must rise

# Missing You

Frightened
and a little strange to myself

as if I'd wakened on the couch
something without a name

I sit down by your absence
I sit by your breath

and draw my best arguments about me
against the empty chairs

I ask myself

'If I close my eyes
will my hands still be wise for you'

The soul remembers in the sense

That pale cloud coasting your arm
the dipper of brown stars between your shoulders

I ask myself

'What time is it by the white daisies in the field'

# Not Quite

It was not quite winter
when we first walked here

The blue air dripped and spattered
The flags of the lookout sweated cold

damp limestone upon stone

Across the river
the trees had banked their wet fires
'God moves in the wind' you said 'If he moves at all'

Today
in this not quite spring

the wind full
the sun like silver birds
flocking the water with its passion

we hunker
against the south sides of stones

warm and animal

# Love's Body

Woman beside me
your hair about my wrist is a rope of honey

And when you touch me with your eyes
with the flower of your mouth
our nakedness makes of itself the naked truth

Marriage is the flesh of our deep delight

I am your own lean animal
the bear sucking the warm fruit of your breasts
the fox at your belly
the hound at your hip

high on the sweet scents of your marrow

Ah wife
stroke the fur of my breath in your lap

As I press my lips to that witches' moss of stiff curl
and kiss your legs with my tongue
tip forth your salts
your delicate ciders
the tenderest silver of the tastes of your body

Pleasure glows at all your proud openings
as you take me into yourself
as you lift yourself toward me like wonder

# Valentine

Your back is a white heart
my prick a stiff flower

I brush your hair
In this dry darkness its sparks fly

Your nipples lift
Your wet bones open their own dark

where every evening takes
its blue beginning

In my hands
I feel the warm moons of your ass rising

Tiny stars of seed
shower

extinguish in the night-room

Woman
fucking you is a race through a long black train

We are two separate leaps of blood

We kiss for breath

# Biography

*for Phil and Peg*

The morning goes by under water

He thinks of his young wife
of her face and body      her voice

On the long dining table
two journals

the red portable
with its lettered fingernails

a packet of fresh envelopes
their edges slashed red and blue

Under the address book
the calendar shows March

the days crossed out through 10

And under these
the notes for a poem

'Hot-dogs by the lake

Water and sky by Whistler

A regatta of angels'

The rest is a scattering of slips      mixed business
A cartridge of spent film

At 5 the sun comes out

the biography of a clean plate
the biography of two Moroccan oranges and a knife

The morning goes by under water
He thinks of his friend who wears a bloodstone
He thinks of his wife

# Hostages

The end of April
Suetonius Paulinus

Blossoming
And still after rain you can see your breath

You must have frozen
your Roman balls off here

And here I am
camped at this fag end of two empires

near walls you built to imprison hostages
hostage to myself

In the square
tulips rich as a clutch of Easter eggs

Chilled bees
sway across the grass

And no one speaks your language
gristle of twenty legions

or for that matter Suetonius Paulinus
mine

*London*

# Elegy for the Duke

Ellington is dead

A-train down from Harlem
Tiger-jawed dashikis flashing down from Harlem

Plum and burgundy and fire

Here
London plays a low-tide blues

Spice of tar
Gulls over brown water

And at the Tate
Turner dissolves us all into pure light

into *Eleanor Rose* and *Argonaut* and *Thames Brittania*

Weather as soul

The world turning over

# Stonehenge: Love in the Ruins

Nothing but eyes
Nothing but bone and tongue

Sprawled survivors
to strip under these prehistoric clouds

Seed
and the light in the grass

flash between your legs
here on this dead man's barrow

and for days
I'll carry your smell on my hands like the sea

Behind us
Stonehenge wrecks

Its heelstone
lunging toward midsummer

In my own country
in another season

I'll kneel before ashes
kindling their fire with my breath

In the evening of each ear
you'll wear

small beads of blood
looped on golden wire

# *Envoi:* July 4th

Down country
Missouri still dreams of plantations

July scorches
to independence and the weather

By dusk
all the pie has been eaten

flies sleep on the ceilings of shadowy verandas
the day slows and softens

Spear by spear
grasses burnt blond

foxtail turned silver
disappear

The painful points
of thickets of leaves are finally dulled

Wild birds
little and fierce

sit singly on fence-wire
or hushed on the one slack power line

and distance sizzles like a damp firecracker
into the oncoming dark

# Starting Out for the Difficult World
## (1987)

# Horses

Horses of earth
Horses of water
Great horses of grey cloud

A blizzard of horses

Dust
and the ponies of dust
Horses of muscle and blood

Chestnuts Roans Blacks
Palominos
Wild dapple of Appaloosa

Spanish ponies
cow-ponies
Broncs Mustángs
Arabians Morgans Tennessee Walkers
Trotters
Shetlands
Massive matched Percherons

Horses
and the names of horses
Whirlaway Man O' War Coaltown
Cannonero
Foolish Pleasure

Horses with tails of smoke

The giddy laughter of horses

Horses of war
their necks clothed in thunder
nostrils wide

The ground beneath them
terrible to look on

Horses of anger
Horses of cruelty
wringing the iron bit in their mouths

The horses of Psyche
Blake's horses
The horses of instruction
Horses of breath

Dawn horses

And the one horse in the heart

that runs
and runs

I

# Starting Out for the Difficult World

This morning, once again,
I see young girls with
their books and clarinets
starting out for the difficult
world. The wind has turned
into the north. It picks a few
leaves from the trees, leaves
already curled, some brown.
They scatter. Even so, their
circles under maple and hack-
berry thicken. The light,
clean as juice to the taste.

Great art, someone said,
rides on the backs of the poor.
Perhaps that's so. But this
is not Long Island. No packed
white waves leap yelping on the shore.
Here, the nights are cold and starry.
Three solitary clouds pig along
the near horizon. And you could
mistake this autumn for Keats's
or your own, or the
autumn of someone you once knew.

# I Used to Think So

The long sigh of steam through pipes,
the air beyond the window, pearly.
                                    Net-
works of stripped branches, and a shag
of spruce.

Upstairs, my heavy colleague
falls toward what monstrousness of flesh?
When a file-drawer rumbles shut,
what righteousness closes on itself?

These are the committees
that grind the heart to powder.

As she leaves,
and the door jerks to a close,
I listen hard into the stillness,
into the building's actual weather,

hearing nothing that loves me,

as if each detail
had to be tricked into meaning.

Outside,
dusk has become reflexive.

The fall of an apple
is the fall of everything,

the sin of gravity.

Seeds, leaves, the child
tumbling from the womb, waterfall and rainfall,
lightfall,

the foot on the stair. . .

What is it once heard
that will not come back in an act of memory

in which the day is as soiled
as the glass of these institutional windows
facing the passion of trees?

To lose it.
Perhaps that's the whole idea after all.

Not to stand
months hence
caught in the doorway of a blue photograph looking
        strange.

I want to start over again
every day of my life.

Do I?
I used to think so.

# I'm Lucky

Sub-zero.
And the birds have lost their talent
for the air.

Back yards
blank with snow. Drifted.
Trampled.

The breath of trees
stripped bare.

My neighbor's blue Maverick
deafens, blind and hub-deep,

on exactly the same spot
he parked it last September.

This wind could cut glass,
freeze your finger to your cheek.

My life is not important.

I understand that.

# All This Way

*On a painting by Edward Levine*

We have come all this way

to an old leather jacket
nailed by its shoulders
to the wall

its scuff
oiled by the sweat of too many hands

The creases the crush

the three plain buttons
that let the front swing open
tell us nothing

tell us it's the kind of jacket
a man might die in

a flag stuffed in one sleeve
in the other dust

Where the lungs were
that hungered for the whip of saw-grass
or burned with the mists of industrial chemicals

where the heart pounded

there is only a blue field
a handful of blurred stars

The belly is a tatter
of red and white bunting
The fist a stump of cloth

Where the head would be
with its marvellous eyes
that loved the roundness of a woman

that saw his daughters
filling out
their first white dresses

that flashed to his boy
banging dirty heels
against the pressed tin of the porch

there
there is only intense darkness

A full pink paper rosebud
its wire stem uncoiling
falls across the left lapel

like a rose of breath

Its color seems to bleed
into the grey wall

washing into it
until we can imagine
the mornings and evenings of our fathers

yours and mine
who were killed early

and who left us these walls
to which they pressed their cheeks

the cheap rooms of their lives
each day
emptying and filling with this light

# Getting It Right

Lightning cracks its red
and green and violet whips,
or sets its white hooks
deep into your soundest sleep,
and you wake.

　　　　　Four a.m.
Towers of air, dark
glaciers you imagine them,
lurch together, avalanching,
rumbling forward under
earth and sill. Rain
scours down in bushels,
or pops off your windows
like a spray of gravel.

Perhaps you get up then,
and let the cat in,
pausing in the unreal flash
to watch the shocked clothes-
line dance and twitch,
trees bucking and blowing
like burnt nerves.

Perhaps you rinse
from the Roumanian crystal
beside the sink
the dark red seal
of last night's wine.

You want to do the next thing right.
You want the storm to go on.
You want it to rain for days
in the avenues of grey churches,
into your hard arms,
as you sleep, and wake, and sleep.

II

# Mnemosyne

Baryshnikov remembers
a sunny day in Latvia

Holding on to his mother's dress
which is chiffon
with yellow and purple flowers

remembers her ash-blond hair
her bright blue eyes

*

The escape artists
are identical twins

and remember each other

*

The three-year-old boy says
'It was red

And very cold'

*

Susan Hansford
summered on Lake Michigan

Her father

afraid of storms
would often embrace her as the clouds darkened

repeating
'How beautiful' 'How beautiful'

*

A trap springs
in the rat-infested grapes

Harry's fingers ribbon with blood

I remember Harry
sweet drunken Harry

# Mineral Point

These immigrant houses
full of clear dry light
face north and east

toward the vanished mouth of the mine

Dressed limestone
And a clear spring
that flows to the kitchen door

where we are told
by a girl whose face
shines like milk
how these Cornish miners
were windlassed by twos
in a wooden bucket

eighty feet down

to drift tunnels
and hack out lead and dry-bone
by candlelight

We have nothing
to love them for

Nothing to forgive

They grew humpbacked

And ate and drank
from tin pails filled with pasty
and water for hot tea

Perhaps they loved their wives

The night
that tumbled down the shafts to them
from Shake Rag St.

like a handful of coin

was the same darkness
that finds us all
naked under our clothes

the same darkness
that chattered beside them
like a stub of black candle

like the starling
in its wicker cage

# Ninety-one in the Shade

*It's not enough to be good...*
*—James Baldwin*

### 1

It's always the same

These swelters of brick or boards
The humid tons of air
Metallic breath of ancient drains

In the kitchen
Flies cruise the centuries of unwashed dishes
Cops cruise the streets

Your third floor Thirties apartment
taken for space and sleeping porches
decays visibly month by month

But your green plants thrive
in this north light

And the moon of your white face
is still beautiful

### 2

After supper

we walk to the bakery
for rolls and black strong bread

or to the laundromat
where our colors gasp and collapse like
television
in the rented glass
of washer doors

The neighborhood
sweats on its dark stoops

Teasing
or pussy-maddened
or weirdo delinquent junkies on a glassy high

In the occasional swing
of headlights
the features of an obscene photograph

where feeling
is the jagged edge of thought

the body
all that keeps us alive

3

Dead black
of morning

And we wake
to the rich burn of ozone
and the distant low batteries of thunder

Lightning
freaks the roaches
from the bedroom floor

I tell you
how sometimes I imagine myself
an enemy soldier

Summer storms
as artillery shelling the city

Naked on the bed

we talk about
whether you think of yourself
as beautiful

about your girlhood

your older sister
who is unhappy

The rain has begun to fall

Clicking in the leaves
beside the window

Puddling the rutted alleys

Then
whistling through the screens
scouring the sills

it monsoons
into the empty streets

cold and foot-wringing

until our windows blur
like the stunned windows in a dream

the endless succession of rented rooms
in which nobody lives

4

Along del Mar
seven days a week

the jag of gas-blue ghost-green letters
and girls

hot-nippled in neon
sizzling on then off then on

Spelling it out

Strain your gut
in the sheep-kill forever

You will never
own a house on the water

Or under the green trees
where time passes quickly

and the wings of butterflies
are dusted a delicate blue

## 5

Our last morning together
you sit on the edge of the bed
stroking a vein in your thigh

Your hair
smells of coffee and eggs

If I kiss you
you will cry

In a vacant lot
where the baked earth blinks with the mercy
of broken glass

a small black boy
tries to get his tail-less kite
to fly

The three of us
tie the rag of my handkerchief to it

And watch it
haul at its saddle-string

tugging the live sail of its colors up
into the hot gust

like a word remembered

that we do not say

# Blue Run

Maxie's Golden Garden Bar
where gorgeous mommies disco
in a glass box, and you tell me
how tough it is—kissing ass
at Harvard and cashing Daddy's
checks. How the best is none
too good, and you're lonely.

Why is it *my* life you think
you want on a dust jacket?
Poetry never saved anyone.

My mother—Dietrich-faced,
Hollywood, Anglo-Irish angel—
died at forty, of pneumonia and
neglect, in rooms above a store.
We were hungry. She was buried
cheap in Roxbury. It was 1934.

Would you move her to richer
ground? Weep for her? Set above
the rack and broken fever of
her bones, marble to give off
light brighter than a star?

And what the hell would you do
with my sister? For whom each day
became one, long, frightened prayer.
And God, a black habit. Can you

mend her orphan's wheedle?

I give you the hand-me-downs,
every old man's shirt I hated,
the shoes that never fit.
And the scorched breath of fields
where I bent and chopped tobacco
until my arms went numb, and my
chest, ribs showing through,
blackened with bitter tar.

It's not for everyone,
                    the drink
of water lifted in the hands:
face wrinkling in the breath,
disappearing—twining, dwindling
between the fingers: sift, pale
oils, invisible codes of salt
dissolving in the blue run and
molten sunlight of the Charles.

# At the Vietnam War Memorial, Washington, D.C.

Today, everything takes
the color of the sun. The air
is filed and fine with it;
the dead leaves, lumped
and molten; flattened grass
taking it like platinum;
the mall, the simple, bare
plan of a tree standing
clothed and sudden in its
clean, explicable light.

And across the muddy
ground of Constitution
Gardens, we've come to find
your brother's name, etched
in the long black muster
of sixteen years of war—
the earth walked raw
this morning by workmen still
gravelling paths, and people
brought here by dreams
more solemn than grief.

A kid in a sweater hurries
past us, face clenched
against tears. And couples,
grey-haired, touching hands,

their midwestern faces calm,
plain as the stencilled names
ranked on the black marble
in order of casualty.
The 57,939 dead. Soldiers,
bag-boys, lost insurance
salesmen, low riders
to nowhere gone no place—
file after broken file
of this army standing at rest.

Were there roses? I can't
remember. I remember
your son playing in the sun,
light as a seed. Beside
him, the names of the dead
afloat in the darker light
of polished stone. Reo
Owens. Willie Lee Baker.
Your brother. The names
of those who believed and
those who didn't, who died
with a curse on their lips
for the mud, the pitiless sea,
mists of gasoline and rain.

In your photograph, it's
1967. June. On the pad
of a carrier, Donald squats
in fatigues, smoking, beside
a rescue chopper, a man
loneliness kept lean;
the sea behind him slurs
like waste metal. He looks

directly at the camera, and
his eyes offer the serious
light of one who's folded
the empty hands of his
life once too often.
Before nightfall, his bird
will go down aslant God's
gaze like a shattered
grasshopper, and the moons
in the rice-paddies cry
out in burning tongues.

All words are obscene
beside these names. In the
morning the polished stone
gives back, we see ourselves—
two men, a woman, a boy,
reflected in grey light,
a dying world among the dead,
the dead among the living.
Down the poisoned Chesapeake,
leaking freighters haul
salt or chemicals. In a grey
room, a child rises in her
soiled slip and pops the
shade on another day; blue,
streaked with high cloud.

These lives once theirs
are now ours. The silver
air whistles into our lungs.
And underfoot, the world
lurches toward noon and
anarchy—a future bright

with the vision of that
inconceivable, final fire-storm,
in which, for one dead second,
we shout our names, cut
them, like these, into air
deeper than any natural
shadow, darker than avenues
memoried in hidden trees.

# To a Cockroach

My cockroach,
my companion.
There is no easy way.

I've seen you drowned
in refrigerated butter.

In New York, one April,
touching a kitchen switch,
I flicked ordinary night
into delirium.
                   All
your old varieties
dizzying the wall
above the pitch and spill
of mouldering dishes.

Hysteria of survival
riding the light.

It comes on us suddenly.
Too quick to be cold.

I loved a girl once
who slammed you dead by half
dozens, night after night,
in a St. Louis railroad
flat. Her big box
of Ohio Blue Tips making

the cheap table silver
jump and ring. Jesus,
she was beautiful!

But you're the perfect
survivor. Twenty-five
million years of humility.

Let's hear it,
tiny jewels of typhoid,
for quickness, aliases:
Shiner. Steam Fly. *Peri-
planeta Americana.*

*La cucaracha, la cucaracha,
ya no puede caminar. . .*
Drunker than artillery.

That girl I loved
I married. And this morning,
the wind lazy in the window
sheers, sheets rich
with the colors of privilege,
coupled jet-fighters
from a nearby air-base
sucking everything up,
every word up
into God's roaring void,
I'm giddy.

Cockroach,
companion,
yours is the life that lasts,
the durable low babble.

Your eyes, quick and dark.
Mine, slow and blue.

# Notre Dame de Paris, 1974

*for Peg*

We give them up
our cities washed in grit

to the whispers of the skin

All but Paris
our grey nun

making a revolution of the rain

a gargoyle
lifting up its stone wing
as if it were an angel's

I see your face
even with my eyes closed

the long banner of your hair

If you would love ugliness
then touch me

Take my anger
to your lips

It will open prisons

It will give a name
to that kiss that spreads its sheer colors

like a bloom of oil
on waters filthy with winter

In the wild belfry
Lady

of this bed
humped and deaf as Quasimodo

ululalia
shaking bone and blood

we ride this ton
of jubilation

banging and banging
together

clapper and bell

# Watching the Nighthawk's Dive

Not even a hawk,
but with a hawk's heart
for the dive—

how many years
of dusks have I watched you,
sucker,

fluttering,
as if short of breath,
to a height,

taking aim
on the wing, then plummeting
toward her,

toward soot
stack, schoolhouse roof, or bare
scatter of gravel,

at the last
second, popping the chute,
riding the umbrella-

strutted, down-
curved wings in a humming
skid,

a Jesus dance,
a soft bronx cheer for the void—
then

climbing again
to dive over and over and over
until the first star's gone

and I can only
hear you,
and the streetlights come on.

I could say
I've loved nothing in this whole, dumb country,
and nobody.

But it wouldn't be true,
brown soul.
—I've loved you.

III

# Bad Heart

So you walk along nowhere—
anybody's beach—the air
a rank chowder of low tide
and you're happy. You'd like
to sew yourself a shirt
out of sunlight. You want
to tell your wife you love
her. And you wait for the
telephone in your ear to ring—.
For an hour. For a week. Is
abstraction a net or a sieve,
Angel? Is an idea a kiss?
A shape such as maples
make unfurling, or willows
falling? Or a steady river
taking up silt and stone,
showing you in a knot or curl,
depth and speed of channel.

And what does it show
if a boat-tail still rudders
in the bucking cross-wind of
your head, where you put it
one green middle-western
afternoon ten years ago,
when you were younger,
and she was very young?

# Key West: Looking for Hemingway

On Mallory Docks
the kids applaud
when the sun goes down

Women
in the hot splash of Key West print

*Cayo Hueso*

where the light gathers
thick enough to breathe

And up at Southernmost
in his air-conditioned room
an off-duty copy sprawls

cooling
in the bruised blue art of his tattoos
veins shot full of lye

The look of the eyes
you would remember    Papa

And the yellow rice
and the black beans and Cuban bread
at the Miramar

Standing here
knee-deep in the shallows

watching the small wahoo holding steady

ghost-fish

I think of you
with your forehead smashed
into perfect prose

plumbing the blue gulf of the Gulf

Behind the *Pilar*
the marlin
breaks water like a great angel

shaking from its sail
a halo of sun-struck brine

And I call out
silently

in a voice you cannot hear

into that terrible
that clear emptiness

where you were

# Nassau: Prince George's Wharf

She points.
Jesús gaffs the yellowtail
from the live box,

nails its head
to the cutting board

and with four quick
strokes of his long,
flexible, blunt knife

guts, gills, and bones it.

Three rags,
three pennants of bright meat
hang from the jaw

he drops
into a brown paper bag.

She pays him
in paper and silver.

She will cook tonight
over charcoal,
with herbs and lemon.

Tomorrow,
beside this same boat,
the sun will school again

on the water.

# Angels And Deaths In St. Augustine

*for my daughter, Arden*

i

The flat four-pointed star
of the Castillo

rises
low on the edge of the bay

A mile distant
spits of sand the Spaniards and English murdered for

a white wing
cruising the strait

ii

In his tourist surrey
an old man

sits black as slavery
under a silk hat

his stump
under a blanket

You shine beside him

through the shaded streets

Past the city gates
and The Ponce de Léon palmed in elegant decay

In the narrow
restored lanes

our horse
breathes like starvation

The man's voice
lifts from the gravels of anguish

the story of each place
each improbable day

*La Señora*
*de la leche*

and some other history
weary as an old blues

The slave market
passed with a word

we step down
tourists still crowding the promenade

You fix to his lapel
the orange carnation you bought from a Hare Krishna

Radiant
you do not kiss his cheek

Overhead
the sky mackerels

the light of this late December afternoon
is pure

At your feet
the Atlantic ebbs

You stand
in a rubble of shells

tearing
a heel of wheat into pieces

The gulls
flash and cry and wheel about you

And pluck your bread
from the water

# On the Public Beach, St. Augustine

Sanderlings. Turnstones. A lone
Willet. Fog-colors morning
sun hasn't yet cut through.
The still cold, grey-green March
Atlantic rolling shoreward flank
after glassy flank. Fraying,
plunging, flattening in its final
scouring rush, to salty lager.
Our old *Sylvan*'s gone, with its
blue-shuttered, wind-scrubbed
weekend cabins. Its tiny
kitchenettes. Wind-white
bedsheets rich with the whiff
of something healing. The quick,
illimitable light. Bulldozed
out for a squat of brown condos.
But the beach is still the public
beach we remember. And we follow
its straggling tidelines like kids,
picking among the strew of broken
arks and angel wings and razors.
The sun lags. But I can't wait
to wade out on the water's
electric chill. The skin buzzes.
The young shine like seraphim
just stepped from their clothes.
Remember how each brisk, incoming
breaker caught our breaths
and lifted us to our toes,

until we took a wet shoulder
and rode it in? Up the beach,
somebody's dog barks like heaven,
flinging itself for joy over
the live backs of the waves.
We laugh, and our talk dwindles
to held hands, as if we perceived,
in body, these things, immediate
and whole. As if we lived, as pure
mathematicians say, on a set
of measure zero, where anything
might happen. At Matanzas, south
of here, *jubilatio* at noon:
shrimp fresh-steamed to crispness
at King's Bait, and eaten from
a plastic cup, their tails tossed
to the complaining gulls. As if
far out from shore, four pelicans
might coast, perfectly echeloned,
long crests and spills of light.
The last time we came here,
in '79, Hurly'd just killed
himself, blown his head open,
back in Iowa, with his god-
damned Smith & Wesson,
the brown corn-stubble essing
easy over the winter hills
like the ancient Chinese character
for river. Now, I no longer
believe we return as birds or fish
or even grit on the heave of the wind.
I think we were never anything
but what we are: the last, lovely,
complex turn of it. And like

the planet, once, and for one
time only. Inventors of this
sea of cloud-struck afternoons,
of heat-haze, the happy dog
of the waves—walking at sun-up
with other strangers this flat
reach of sand, and smiling
occasionally, back at them
as they pass. Saying, occasionally,
"Good morning. Good morning."

# Black Angel

The wind walks past my window again
wearing a dress of green leaves.
I look up. But no one's there.
I'm studying *A Field Guide to Wild-*
*flowers.* I've just discovered
the tall, spiky ones on my back
slope, the ones with heads of tiny,
pink, rattler mouths are woodbane,
and it seems to make a difference.
I'm curing herbs. Rose smell
of pepper. Pepper of fresh basil.
And here in the old root cellar
where I write, one good sentence
makes a difference. And Barber's
*Adagio For Strings.* The opening
of de Boisvallee's *Religioso.*
This poem is an adagio. A slow
yearning of winds and strings.
Like the hot August night I got
drunk with friends, and laughing
and sweating, we linked arms and lay
back in the deep wine, the cool
Einstinian space of summer grass,
streaming upward like angels,
past trees, past crumbling eaves
and stars, rising like music farther
and farther out the closer home.
So I'm checking the rue, the rose-
mary, the sweet marjoram. I'm closing

the book of flowers. All stories
yearn and sing, Rodina Feldevertova,
and that makes a difference.
The parsley will smell of England;
the oregano and basil of Greece;
the rosemary remind us of heaven.
They say you died, mysteriously,
at seventeen, homeward bound
on an Italian liner. Now, you stand,
larger than life, over your own grave
—the famous Black Angel of Iowa City—
the iron cape of your wings
spreading its perfect shadow in perfect
sunlight, the right one pointed
upward to protect us, the left
touching the earth, to gather us in.

# Now

You come over a hill, suddenly,
late afternoon or early evening
on 6A to Beach Point. Provincetown
to Long Point Light, a yellow,
dissolving Venice by Whistler
or Monet. Bay flat. Silver
grey. Dark blue further out.
I'm not talking about the past.
I'm talking about my sister,
my wife, myself—all of us
travelling without reservations.
I'm talking about three small
sails tacked on the far horizon.
At Shoreline Village, cabins
1930's, sixty bucks a night
and twenty yards from salt water,
my sister talks about shells.
Sister Whine. Sister Twinkle.
Fifty years a nun this spring
and all No to my Yes. A taste
for dull food, and expensive
Irish whiskey in her tea. Next
door, our neighbors play volley-
ball without a net, their little
girls shrieking like sea-birds.
Danielle. Michelle. Julie.
I'm not talking about childhood.
I'm saying when the tide here

goes out its long mile at dusk,
the bay's a wet barnyard where
a dozen boats strand and heel over,
and clammers rake the golden muck
for steamers. Later, the years
come down slowly like stars
on Mama's West Dennis or Harwich
or wherever we summered the fall
she died, hundreds of herring-fry
shoaling and sparkling in a bright
terror of shallows, my sister's
beads clicking in the night. I'm
not talking now about memory,
but the way words leap backward
to their beginnings, Wittgenstein's
"significant silences," his desk
drawer of posthumous phrases,
words detached into mystery
on little scraps of blue paper.
So the clear argument of morning
comes on, and lovers rise
from their rented beds to lie
in the sun. In Commercial Street,
one man receives from another
"the signature of God" in his hand.
"What is it?" I ask my wife.
A talisman? A smooth stone?
A word from Hebrew cast in silver?
I lay back on the sand of this
rough prayer of a beach and close
my eyes on the four white ribs
of the sky, listening to the low
roll of surf say *"jour," "jour,"*
and sometimes *"toujours"* to the shore.

IV

# What the Stones Know

Fire says
"The flesh. The flesh."

Water says
"Hair."

The air says
one or two feathers in a field of wheat.

Earth says
"Sweat."

The mowing
dazzles with the shadows of passing clouds.

I say to my son,

"Write your name
on everything that's yours."

# Driving the Coeur d'Alene Without You

Rain shadows the lake,
and the road curves away and then back,
back and then up, and the sun
appears and disappears.

Below,
the knifetip flash and white wing-dip of mainsails,
the blue of sunburst spinnakers.

In a green fjord,
a canopied motor launch turns the water back
in two icy curls from its prow.

I tell you,
the dumb stain on my shirtpocket
could pass for loneliness.

I want it over quickly.

One by one,
the bays go by: Beauty, Turner, Bell. . .
and long,
dusty constellations of mountain asters.

At Powderhorn,
I pass a family of three
picking berries.

The woman
a print dress in the brambles.
The man hardly glances up.

Their boy stands
stock still in his faded, dirt-stained t-shirt,
watching me pass,

his eyes solemn with worry
like the eyes
of any young, wild thing.

At Harrison Flats,
the sky is cut by wires, and a combine
dies in a stubblefield.

I am numb.

I drive on
toward the house I live in
that is not mine,

and where,
so that I will never feel shame,
so that I will not dream,

you left
stalked and whiskered heads of wheat
in a ripple-glass pitcher

beside the door.

# On a View of Paradise Ridge from a Rented House

Crest and body
feathered dark with pines,

its wheatstubble right wing
stroking downward,

it holds its slow, hooked
glide toward winter.

A stray hackle of smoke
drifts back, dun and grey,

where a field is burning.
The evening light is dry,

a light that is nothing
that makes all things real.

Behind me, a great
wall of glass trembles.

I can taste my own blood,
strong as coffee,

dark as this furious burgundy.

# North of Steptoe Butte

The feel of your body
carries me with it
mile after falling mile.

The roll of these hills.
No one's dream of you.

Yellow dustdevils whirling
above a field of wheat.
White horse on a hillside.

That singleness repeated.

Where pure mind is only
wind banging and yattering
through open truck-windows.

Number brushing bone.

And your hair
drifting in bright waves across this sheet
of blue space.

# Written in Winter

The clustered orange
berries of mountain ash
are belled with snow.

The tree itself
templed with winter.

The others, tufted,
boled, and battened.

The most distant,
clouded like a breath
of frozen steam,

the miles of ground
everywhere, zillioned
with crystals.

Here, in the bright
zeroes of this air,
nothing happens.

But later,
your nostrils burn,
your teeth ache.

And all night
you ask the children
of the world

to forgive you.

V

# A Short History of the Middle West

Under this corn,
these beans,
these acres of tamed grasses,

the prairie still rolls,

heave and trough,
breaker and green curl,

an ocean of dirt tilting and tipping.

Its towns
toss up on the distance, your distance,
like the wink

of islands.

And the sky
is a blue voice
you cannot answer for.

The forked and burning wildflowers
that madden
the ditches

nod without vocabulary.

Your neighbor
is out early this morning—the air
already humid as raw diamond.

Drunk or lonely,
he's scattering large scraps of white
bread for the birds

as if it were winter.

He'd give you the sour undershirt off
his back—
sweet, bad man.

Does he remember
rain salting down from that flat, far shore
of clouds

slowly changing
its story?

On this shore,
the trees all babbling with their hands?

# Wichita

If there's no winter here,
it's only for lack of snow.
Take a meadow abandoned to real
estate, the real estate abandoned
to grass and weed; the sky, zinc;
the north wind, iron, and banging,
sliding, down the shadows
of wheel-ruts, down the long
double lane of trees
that lead to no abandoned farm-
house, no tumbled foundations;
the way just stopping dead
at the swampy crossing
where newer tracks cut through.
There, we're left to do
what we can with the hawk
driven off by a crow, the couple
of pines flanked south,
and the rose-bush, run wild and
tough in the pale sun, flashing
rose-hips bright as any petals.
You get this like a slow post-
card from one of those tropical
countries, the view fixed
in one corner in the window
of the stamp: cheap, exotic, vivid.

# Everything Else You
# Can Get You Take

Hay and panic grass
combed into rolling windrows.
Minstrel-faced sheep. A few
head of cross-bred Charlies.

No place we ever imagined
we'd be. No sea's edge
where a low wave sputters,
ignites like a fuse, and races
hissing along the shore.
No thin, viral mist fizzing
the windshield, gorges rising
grey as China in the rain.

Only this long roll of
space where day-lilies
leap any breaks in the fences,
flooding down ditches, orange
against the many colors of green,
—only the jingle and ring of
morning crickets in the dew.

Don't ask how long we've
been here, or why we stayed.
You fall in love with
a climate. Everything else
you can get you take.

# Heat

The valley brims with it.
Steamy sea-floor
of trees where small birds
swerve and dart like fish.
God's old ocean of grey air,
where a lone crow rows,
slow and steady, toward
home, or nowhere in particular,
on strong, black oars.

# True Story

What does the morning say
I wish I hadn't heard before,
the wind still for the first
time in days, the little maple
standing like sodden bronze
beside the garden. Beneath
it, the green roses of the cabbages
unfold, zucchini spread the
canopies of their first true
leaves.
       Tell me again how your
uncle Willie sold his acre
of downtown Wichita for five
bucks and a shot of booze.
And how, where oil-rockers
dipsy-doodle in the wheat,
fire of sex or soul could fry
a young girl's hair to ringlets.

If the rich talk only
to the rich, then it's true:
we are whatever's left of us.
In the scrub, the cardinal
whistling like a rubber mouse.
But nothing's so exotic here
as the emptiness of ordinary
day. It falls through the eyes
of my cat, turning slowly, like
flakes of sunlight in the air.

# Blood Harvest

Say "Goodbye." Say whatever
you want. Summer here begins
like thirty years of trying
to breathe under water.
                         Blue
corn surging the plumped lap
and sow-belly hills. Sweat.
Nights rinsed in hot moonlight.

The farmer who looks at you
and crumbs dirt from under
a thumbnail black as cake.

You don't leave it. You
give two fingers to a whirling
gear, your children to the
church. Slash lips and tongue
and arms until blood rains
on the harvest, tasselled and
feathered and green as
the dumb god of the grass.

# Victor

A farmhouse left to high
grass. Clapboard grey-
white as wind-scoured bone.
The mouth of the doorway,
the eye of one window
battered shut. So many
stories gibbering in and
out of this empty head
like shadowy small birds.
We see it at 186,000
miles a second, the speed
light travels from even
a vanished star. Victor
out back in his vegetable
garden. His raked and
stained fedora. Scrubbed
knuckles of young potatoes
bubbling up under his hoe.
His woman calls him into
the fading house for supper,
the spider by her window
riding out the wind in its
harness of silk, light in
the trees coming and going.
But Victor stays, watching
the bright air of evening
rain down, bloom, fill.

# They Know the Beautiful Are Risen

Old Hog-Eye. Feedlot pig-
god, and back forty eater
of children, snuffles down
the happy mud of heaven,
his great sow swilling it
together with the bright eye
of a butcher weighting scales.
Bacon or sausage. Ham.
Hocks for beans. Pickled
trotters. And years of
being in bad with the Jews.

Is there ice in the glove
in the sty? The wallow
of rich slops for curly
tails and bright tusks
her root eye opens, his stump
of brain shocks and sparks
from juicy channels, exactly
like any other story
that dies each night
when the sky burns down?

Figure it out.
They know the beautiful are risen.

# Ark & Covenant

Chip, chirr, blabber, whistle, hingey
squeak
of spring birds—.

We all know what that means.

Lawns patched and clotted
with snow.
Shadows and the late sun slanting.

I hardly ever speak
my own language any more.

My mouth fills with silence.

With a useless kiss.

Nothing
to devil the restless ear. Nothing
to sign

on the clear and solemn air.

What I Think I Know
*New Poems*

# Five Short Complaints

### 1 *The Children's Hour*

Rm 5129. Two empty
beds. 5130. Eric
Gonzalez, king of
two a.m., ruptured
appendix, pops side-
wheelies into his room
in his silver chair.
5132. Randy. Wild
Mongol pony, going
deaf. 5133. Robbie
L—, turning a corner
on spinal meningitis.
5136. A handful of
baby in an oxygen tent.
This is the way
it begins for a lucky
few. And we all know
how it ends, right?
But better. Harder.

### 2 *Eighty-four Days Without Rain*

Each day, dawn—
and the scorched penny
of the sun coppery
already in the white
sky, fields
bitched and brown,

topsoil stone dry
ten inches down
under even the deepest
oaks. Two days
now, they've dragged
the river below
the old power-dam
for the body of the boy
who slipped away there
last Friday night
trying to keep cool.
Bindweed shrivels
in this heat. Late
morning markets rise
and fall. Pray
for an hour of shadow,
a thimbleful of rain.
We stunt and wither
and die upward from
the roots like gods.

## 3   Mercy

I watch the red-tail
stoop into the long
weeds beside the road
and come up empty.
Half of all hawks starve,
wear their wings out
trying to stay alive,
the way countless
grass consumes the wind,
the way we wear
our lungs out, crying.

## 4   *Finch*

Beyond anyone's will
words dream. Just
as misery drives us
out of ourselves. Just
as, when I cut open
this pear and bite
into it, I taste
in its meat a sweet
wind blowing, cold,
—gritty with snow.

Finch, you had class,
your green eyes
focussed into cracked
bits, your abortion
screaming in the closet.
I still remember
your understudied Portia.
Raspy contralto. Elegant
in the luscious strut
of your own parade.

Now, driving this
waste of freeway west,
sky clear, the sun
in its pink-gold aura
setting like the orange
on a Sunkist label,
I believe in the unforeseen.
Nothing you believe in.
In the green shade,

the birds chattering
and barking and singing
in the air. And the
air. Nothing more.

## 5  *What I Think I Know*

Clipping the dirty
quarter-moons
of my fingernails,
watching them
fall through space
into the tangle
of my wastebasket,
I think I know
this whole day—
this earth, its human
histories; brute,
bird, and blood;
the sea, fruit,
air, the hot
stars; the woman
moving from room
to room—may all
be whistling
in a single cell,
smaller than virus,
or the rat's gene
for long life;
adrift in stupid
grace, in a wild,
improbable breathing.

# "How Pure a Thing Is Joy"

*for Peg*

It's not the fact,
it's the feeling.
The cat jack-knifed
into sleep at your feet.
The struck match
flaring like a dancer.

There's no beauty
like your great human beauty.

Well, keep it light,
I tell myself, knowing
there must be days when
my kiss weighs a ton
and even delight tires,
and praise, when the last
thing you want, probably,
is another metaphor.
And you're right.

This marriage is a grace,
flawed and outrageous,
we lift each day from
the smash-up of the world.

Before first light,
before a scratch of sun
explodes in the torn shade,
I waken, often, in your
arms, loving still
your still sleeping,
night-searching self,—
listening to the steady
whirring of the cat
who thinks she's you.

# Aquamarine

Downrange from LeJeune,
gutted missile tracking
towers; hints of cordite
and jet-fuel on the sea-
wind. North Topsail's
mile-wide strip of old
government issue bleached
the color of summer chino.
Beach a flat, brown bake
at ninety-eight degrees.
We shell before breakfast,
washing the morning's haul
in the kitchen sink. Dull
Atlantic cockles mostly;
a Baby's Ear; one perfect
Lion's Paw; a few, small,
bright calicoes my sister
wouldn't walk so far for,
just as she won't sketch
swimmers, or the jeweled hues
of the blue crab I hold up
for her by one of its fire-
tipped claws, or recall
from deep space the years
before my mother's death,
the voice I can't remember.
"Those weren't nice times,"
she says. I stand there,
looking out over the sea,

listening to the surf's white,
ruffled, incessant hush;
thinking how, in a few
days, a surgeon will open
my throat for the second
time in three years and
make me wise, if plastic
tubing carrying away
the body's dark fluids,
or drugged grief is wisdom.
This morning, I'm brave
and dumb as those young
chopper jocks we watched
last night, practicing
blind landings from the
carrier moored off shore.
Dumb as sunlight on these
red and yellow umbrellas,
or the waves that wrap
the pale shoulders of my
beautiful, young wife in
a gown of shining froth.

# You

When I think
of the simple
fact of you
walking there,
I see the coming
on of long red-
gold afternoons
over the sea;
the long, even
longer evenings;
blue-purple and
black-green skies
going down
in a slow, silver
sweat of stars
on the Gulf of Mexico.

# Estero Island Beach Club

By day, they lie
beside the heated,
turquoise pools,
tanning to the look
of imported leather;
at evening, gathering
beachside on the terrace
to celebrate a sun
going down gold off
Sanibel and Captiva.
Businessmen, retired
farmers and their wives,
bearing a eucharist
of chips and dip;
nachos smothered
in Wisconsin cheddar;
olives of California
cardboard packed
in water. Booze
for the blood of Christ.
They talk mostly
of money, reckoned
in hundred thousands;
of acres of land;
plats, accesses;
strings of hot-dog
stands; the old
joke about the guy
who puts a twenty

in the collection plate
and takes out change.
Back in Illinois,
the farmhouse is modern.
No longer the flaking
shit-kicker cold
enough in winter
away from the wood-
burning stove to stop
your breath, in summer,
muggy as a sponge,
and smelling sickly
sweet of peonied
wallpapers, milk,
and manure. Behind
the barn, the White
Diamond silo tilts
in the air like
something Italian;
the colors of early
spring are Tuscan—
umber and ochre
under a breath of slip.
Hours later, passing
two vagrant kids
sleeping on a stolen
blanket, I'll still
hear them, these
voices raw-tongued
and democratic,
speaking without apology;
and the moon will rise
silvery over a talc
and powdered sugar

beach, and the Gulf
breeze strike softly
across the bright
praise of waters.

# These Days

I don't stay in town long.
I drive out to Race Point—
bright stunt kites, diving
and sailing in the stiff, north
wind, and people walking
the beach. The sea's sunny
and dark. I drive on, down
to Herring Cove, park,
and walk the beach myself.
A man and woman are fishing.
"What do you catch here?"
I ask. "Blues," the man
says. "Bass sometimes,
but mostly blues," he says.
"How's the fishing been?"
"Good," the woman says.
"We was down Whaddyacallit?
—Highland? High Point.
A guy had five blues. Big."
Her hands measure off four
feet of air. "Well, good
luck," I say, and move on.
It's the end of the season,
and back at East Harbor—
if I write this in French,
will it be clearer? In Spanish,
will it be more passionate?
You're reading a translation.
The beach is empty. High

cirrus and a scrap of lemon
on blue sky, and salt-grass
Thoreau named *psamma arenaria*
for its love of sand when
Nauset was desert. I'm swirling
my wind-chilled whiskey
in its glass, and watching the sun
collapse in heaven-fire,
or wild glory, or whatever
passes for that these days.

# This Isn't a Story

This isn't a story
I want to tell, or need
to. I've shoveled
the night's hard snowfall
from the drive and heaped
it, mail-box high,
for the neighbor kids
to stomp over. I've fed
the squirrels and put out
black sunflower and wild
wood seed for the birds—
the female cardinal rose
and dusky and black
in the crisp morning sun.
I've written the necessary
letters, made a couple
of phone-calls, watered
the fig-tree, the impatiens,
and the passionate azalea
my wife sent yesterday
to lift my Valentine
heart. My daughter's
marriage is in trouble.
There's no story at all,
really. Just this snapshot
of my father, my mother's
lover, hand in pocket,
two-tone shoes, a car—
maybe the black '32

Buick—parked behind him
under dusty trees
in a dusty lane. Just
this photo, lost
for years and now returned—
crumpled, cracked, its
lower left-hand corner
gone. Yellowing, as old
box-Brownie pictures do.

# Hard Souls

Nuthatch,
titmouse,
chickadee—
one after the other
at the window feeder,
and where winter
suet ripens
in the wild cherry,
a downy ladders
the red netting.
All morning
every morning,
sun or snow,
the constant glide
and swoop and braking
of wings, ceaseless
picking and stabbing
of small, strong
beaks, murmur
and twit of souls
hard beyond
will or desire,
quickening my neighbor's
garden of collapsing
bed springs
and old ranges
abloom with rust;
fenders snarled
in weeds and barb-wire.

Little breaths
of summer dust
leapt up among
sunflower and thistleseed
into angelness,
what stroke powering
reach and wing,
ravishing the starved
air, these bright
tons of gravity.

# A Capella

I'm standing here in the church
of oaks and hickories, in the chapel
of winter mulberries and leafless
cherries. In the church of the long,
dry creek akindle with moonlight
on snowmelt. I'm standing here under
Mercury and Venus, under Cepheus
and Cassiopeia, under the dark vault
of the dragon and the bear, getting
cold in this cold cathedral of stars,
warming my blood with whiskey, my
hands in a little chapel of smoke.
I'm standing at the shrine of Our
Lady of the Sunday night steak
and the broiled potato, the Virgin
of mixed greens and crusted bread.
Tart saint of Chardonnays and tall
Bordeaux and peppery Burgundy.
I'm standing here thinking about
the perfect emptiness of it;
of the warmth that will touch me
when I open the door and see you
at dinner by firelight in this
house we built with our own hands.

# Daylilies

Midsummer, and my neighbor's
cutting weeds in the dusk—
doilies of Queen Anne's Lace;
wild, white morning glories.
Our cherry tree is dying,
probably of chemicals or drought.
All day, the wrens have been
in it, trembling and bubbling.
Two blocks north of here,
they're tearing out the canopy
of oaks and hickories, little
umbrellas of mulberry; paving
the woods to build houses,
a beach, a nine-hole golf course.
The business of business.
Piper Alpha still burning
in the North Sea; soldiers
smashing the hands of young men
in Jerusalem, Johannesburg.
Where are the poems of the ant
and the dog, the assault rifle's
immaculate lines, music in
the breath of a blown rose?
It's nearly dark now, and I
haven't photographed the day-
lilies: Red Admiral, Emma Sue
Dean, Chicago Fire. The first
star's cruising that widening
hole in the sky. O backbreakers

of the world! In the fury
of pure song, nothing endures,
and there's no consolation.

# Moment in Late Summer

The month is August,
but the day is October,
and under the overhang
of this expensive house,
the windsock's rainbow
colored tentacles
dawdle like a cuttle-
fish's in the bright,
dry breeze. A boy
I've never seen before,
whose mother loves
him too well for his
sweet, uncomplicated
face; the new, warm
smell of his hair,
is skateboarding
past my window
on his way to somewhere.
And I know, out back
in Paradise, our wrens,
feeding their late
second brood, are fierce
as dogs; the tiny,
wild cherries, turning—
yellow to red to black.
I'm sick of importance.
The world is sick
to death of importance.
But what can I do?

And should I? Should I?
All night long for years,
I've rattled this cage
of stars, troubling
your deepest sleep.

# In the Gardens of Fabulous Desire

39, west of Hollandale,
a sharp, backward curve
and you miss it, the small
house set in deep shade;
lion and swan and tower
rising from the burnt grass.
No scene from childhood,
unless yours, like mine,
was a long, bad dream.
When you kill your engine
and step down in the rutted
gravel, and pass finally
under the dark pines,
you'll feel the hair lift
on your scalp a little,
absent eyes watching
from behind dimity curtains
brittle with dust and sun.
But the cheesemaker whose
house this was—grey stucco
studded with bits of bottle
glass, pastel Fiestaware,
fragments of mirror—he's
dead now. His woman, gone.
Sons moved on to Sheboygan
or Monroe. Nothing left
but this house and its gardens
of fabulous desire. Blond
Snow White, breasts

swelling under her scallop-
shell bodice. The Viking
in his griffin-prowed skiff,
beached and listing, summer
after summer, further
into the glacial earth. It
may come to you like the cry
of children playing out
of sight across a green ravine.
Or distant as the jumble
of sleepy bees, hum of flies,
gorged with musky blackberries
beyond the milkhouse—what
are our calloused hands,
leaky bladders, and bad backs,
but drunken song? Our ruined
faces, but work? And you
may think if you could get
the words to ring down
right, like Neptune's Wheel,
noun, verb; noun, verb;
the clown under his pointed
cap, the owl, the boy reading,
noun, verb—this whole
Calliope of crumbling dream
would wheeze again, whirl
and sing in the wild heat
and stagger of these weeds.

# Plenty

If I could speak in any
one of the three voices
of the dolphin, light
would certainly be one
syllable, and grace another.
And I'd tell that story
in which God's his own
orphan, standing alone,
without shoes, at the dark
tops of the trees, amid
the wild, slow luminousness
of a hundred fireflies
floating, rising, shooting
off suddenly across
what's left of the night,
like soft stars. But
mine is this common
tenor, boozy with wine
and late summer at Rueil,
the path running out
in a rush of green;
the house touched by sunlight;
bench, empty; the small,
round, marble-topped table
with its jug of clear water
and red roses, green.
Red roses everywhere.
Listen, I say, it's plenty.
Let's put our feet up

on these chairs, tip our
crazy heads back in the sun
under the Chinese elms,
the dogwoods, the mulberry—.
Let's be kings
of the earth awhile.

# Acknowledgments

Five poems included here have never before appeared in book form. "The Way We Live Now" first appeared in *The American Poetry Review;* "Nassau: Prince George's Wharf" in *National Forum;* "In a Fugitive Season" in *Snapdragon;* "Pop: At Checkers" in *The West Coast Review* (Canada); and "North of Steptoe Butte" in *Willow Springs.*

Of the new poems in this volume, these have appeared in the following magazines: "Daylilies" and "How Pure A Thing Is Joy" in *Folio;* "Hard Souls" appeared in *The Georgia Review;* "Plenty" and "You" in *Practices of the Wind;* "Aquamarine" in *Shenandoah;* "The Children's Hour," "Eighty-Nine Days Without Rain," "Mercy," "Finch," and "What I Think I Know" in *Manoa* under the title "Five Short Complaints;" "Moment In Late Summer," "These Days," "This Isn't A Story," in *Ploughshares;* and "In The Gardens Of Fabulous Desire" in *Western Humanities Review.*

# About the Author

Robert Dana was born in
Boston in 1929, and has
lived in Iowa for many
years, where he is
poet-in-residence at
Cornell College. The
author of eight books of
poetry, he has served as
distinguished visiting poet
at four universities
and was awarded
a National Endowment
Fellowship in 1985.
Mr. Dana's work won
The Delmore Schwartz
Memorial Award for
Poetry in 1989.